Winners never quit!

Hard learned lessons
by
a rookie salesman

ISBN 978-1-4466-1758-8

Dedicated to all those great people
that gave me opportunities
to grow and learn
as a professional and as a person

Preface

Who is this guy?

I am just like you. I am a hardworking modest salesman wanting to do better. I am always on the look out on how to be better.

I am also an aerospace engineer that very early on his career was more attracted to business than to sitting behind a CAD station or programming some aerodynamics code. After some years in the aerospace industry through various roles, you may start to feel comfortable and under control and one day, you go into the commercial world...and you're a complete rookie!

When you're a rookie, like in many things in life, you are full of energy and confidence, and hopeful that everything will turn out great.

I have not lost the energy and confidence levels, but suddenly realized how much of a rookie I was and how many hard learned lessons I've been through and for sure many more will follow in the coming years.

This book is about sharing. I share with you what I have learned so far with no reserves whatsoever.

I don't claim to make you better, faster or that I know of methods you haven't heard of or supported by year and years of research of experiment.

I personally have had enough of the 12 rules for... 99 rules to liberate you, 21 ways to make you...and EVERY single book says YOU can learn even if you're not a born leader, salesman, athlete or chess player. It's like watching TV shop. All claim to make you thinner, toned up and more attractive. Maybe. Maybe there's too much good advice and research out there. So don't be disappointed if you see the numbers of chapters are not a finite number of rules, but just the total of ideas grouped in a way that makes sense to me, while I am sharing with you.

OK, so why the hell do I write this book then? In a naïve way, I want to share the fun and excitement of learning to do your job everyday. Experimenting, feeling excited, anxious, and sad, tired and pushing sand uphill.

My approach to writing this book is not reading half of Amazon's books and giving it my twist. The more management books you read the more you understand this. And what can you say, good ideas are good ideas, no one can argue against that. But I want mine to be different. I did not find any new principles or investigated for years. I just wrote down my reflections from my limited experience and some examples. As simple as that, so read it and enjoy learning from a normal guy. Otherwise, close it and get out of my book.

About this book

(Pink Floyd – Learning to fly)

This book is a series short stories and experiences from the point of view of an engineer that had to learn how to do it. By doing it I mean selling. By doing it I mean moving the business forward. It's not something you can learn by just reading (you can of course read books like these), but you need to practice. Like golf, you may know all about the swing, the rules and the gear, but if you don't go to the course and try hitting it well, your chances are, to put it mildly, very slim. I write this book not with the intention to teach you, the aspiring or not, young or old salesman, but to warn you of what lies ahead, what worked for me, and also lots of things that did not.

Moreover it's about how I have learned many times the hard way (never the easy way) on being better, more effective and achieving some progress in the process of selling your ideas, your services. So I don't claim to have the ultimate success or made millions out of it. Just a lot of experiences, some small some big, but all of them learned on the job. I am, in a way, as someone much wiser than me once said, understanding my life backwards and living it forward.

It's not a cook book or a "you can learn" these skills. If you don't like selling, there is nothing wrong with that. Go read about gardening or cooking. While I can't claim to be overly successful or have done years of field research, anyone interested in salesmanship will almost immediately agree to the ideas and principles.

Talking to a close friend, he admits he thinks it's unfair other people have better salaries just because they managed to sell themselves better. I was shocked to hear this, not because I did not know it, but because he, as a great engineer, did not see it coming. We are all into selling!

Cliché, I know, but you will feel it in your own skin, if you haven't already. So, get it in your head once and for all that it's like that. How you do it is another matter, therefore my sharing with you of the knowledge I have acquired so far.

Without trying to offer a sales model or any sort of framework, this book first looks at some of the major things a salesman must do:
- Aim: You need to know what you want from whom. If you just "shoot" at anything passing by you will lose a lot of energy and focus
- Being prepared: You can never be too prepared. The world is not getting simpler or easier and it's up to you to keep up. This means covering the most aspects you can with rigor and discipline
- Following up: It's never a "fire and forget", or any other sort of passive tactics. It's quite the opposite, you really need to insist, ask again and again and follow up on every presentation, lead, conversation or proposal.

- Relationships: Although it is in the middle of the book, it is central to the key messages in this book. It's about people, how you interact with them and managing your networks
- Making it happen: This may very well be "the edge" to many salespeople. Excellent strategies and well defined targets are only good as long as someone is executing them. You will find plenty of literature on the execution topic and they will all agree with this: it differentiates good intentions from good sales & business development
- You the salesperson: In the end of the day you are a person doing your job. A special job, in its own way, and with its particularities, again like any other. I offer you my perspective from one that was in it up to its neck
- Finally, "Never forget" is an assortment of lessons to bear in mind. No more no less.

Throughout the book I will offer some real life examples and stories (no references or names, sorry) to illustrate that particular point.

Just to break the mould, and being a music addict, let's make this more fun and I've added a suggested soundtrack to the book. Each major point has a song which is related to the text and, at least for me, it reminds me what that is all about!

Aim

Aiming well is perhaps half of any strategy. After all, how do you expect to hit the bulls eye if you don't know where to shoot?

It really depends on if you're aiming to grow business on existing products and services, or expanding into new territories and technologies.

Do you know what you're doing?

(Nik Kershaw – The riddle)

It can be very frustrating for you and the top management when results are not quick and the short term prevails. While I have been lucky to not have someone breathing down my neck constantly (although with all fairness is a mild help), there may be times that questions will surface about the speed and effectiveness of the sales cycle. Here are the basic steps:

1. You cannot sell to those that do not know you or what your company offers
2. Even if they know you, they might not need your services
3. Even if they need your services, this may not be the best timing
4. Even if they do need it and it's the best time, competition looms and will not give up the business without a fight
5. And finally, you may bid and lose out. So hang in there for the next one. Go to step 1.

As you can see, there is a chain of "even if" that may take some time to materialize in a contract. This is a reflection of the sales pipeline. Also it illustrates the importance of staying in contact as circumstances change and you may get that break you've been dreaming of.

The pipeline

(Faith no More – A Small victory)

Before you go crazy selling your products and services, you need to think about the pipeline. Pre-sales is feeding that pipeline of opportunities aggressively so that you end up with lots of options, contacts and potential partners.

The pipeline can be seen or organized in many ways. You may have a lot of known people across an industry or industries, but not much going on.

From those which I assume are plenty (if not, you need to get a networking strategy fast), some of them will be sales leads, opportunities and ideas to find partners to collaborate. Of those, a few will become RFPs or RFQs, and even fewer will become finalists in the race for winning a big contract. Finally only those surviving all the above will be merited with a contract award. Not over yet.

Contracts negotiations can be complex, can break down or not getting to an agreement in the end. It's not over until it's over, and that means ink to paper from whoever in your organization signs the contract. At this point you are allowed to have a drink :-) So cheer up for every small victory, in the long run they will become larger and more visible.

All stars lined up

It's that time when all stars are lined up and things seem to go smooth (not so many times to be honest). I still struggle with aiming for this, most of the time it is half strategy half crystal ball.

It's also called pre-sales where you try to anticipate the moves of the client, competitors and important steps.

If you work in a long cycle industry like aerospace where things can take years or close to a decade, you may think there's plenty of time to think through how to get to that deal (by the way, your competition is at least thinking the same).

It's like that ad for a German car, time is so relative depending if you're having fun (your idea of fun may vary wildly in this context).

It can go very fast when you're lining up what's going on, who's on it and how do I get that invite, or slowly, painfully slowly when waiting to see what's the final bidders list.

Lining up the stars can be matching what you hear about what's going on the in the market with what you aim to do in the future. You now have an end point to aim. It's the in between bit that's tricky!

Focus (really!)

It may be your company is trying to "sell sand in the desert" or that you have so many interests that you lose sight of the final aim.

So get to grips and focus, I mean really do it. Have a vivid picture of the "NOW", what can you offer and what references and projects you have under your belt.

Do not mix with the aspirations or areas you would like to enter (see chapter about past, present and future).

You should and need to be updated about your sector and the world in general, but don't over do it, it is so easy to get dragged onto reading newspapers, RSS feeds, magazines, etc that you may start to lose focus on the execution. Don't try to draw the perfect snapshot with all the data just to make that first phone call. As you will see in the next chapter, being prepared is essential, I am just warning of you going crazy about it.

If you do exhaustive business intelligence about your competitors and then you don't read it or don't use it, stop now. What is the use of all those reports, numbers and factoids if they all add up to you trusting your gut?

A pitch of past, present and future

(Huey Lewis – Back in time)

You may have done it many times with the best of intentions and even without realising you were. Sometimes presentations are a mix of past experiences, present projects and future aspirations.

While as a salesman this may sound perfectly normal and correct, one day you will be a customer and you will see it differently, so when that happens remember this feedback for the next time you put some slides together.

As a potential customer one day, a very young company describes in too much detail the amount of projects they have experience. At a point in time it was very confusing as I knew they could not possibly have done all of that in just one year, and for sure it must include experiences from their whole careers before these salesman were entrepreneurs selling me their company expertise. Further ahead in the presentation you bump into a list of many aspects related to a possible product, more of a wish list, supposedly backed by the previous experience.

Now you may be very aware of the mix, but also confused. You want to know what they CAN provide, not what they wish they could, or find out that they claim so much experience, but not of their OWN.

I take the feedback as customer and apply it next time I am pitching. People most of the times want exact references and actual facts, and can be a real turn off if it ends up being a brain dump of your past life and future aspirations.

It's better to sell ONE good skill or expertise with proper back up material than to fire in all directions. Even if you're starting and may think it maximizes your chances of success, I can guarantee it will only turn off the customer. You will know it too if you have been one.

So preparing your pitch and iterating it over and over is one of the best things you can do. It focuses the mind, it surfaces inconsistencies and will give you insights for the next time around you have to deliver it.

Be prepared

Never a motto such as "Be prepared" was more adequate to a salesperson. At the rate of change companies and people are experiencing these days; one cannot let himself not be ready.

The game

(Kenny Loggins – Danger Zone)

If you feel that sometimes it's a game, well it's sort of. The problem is when you don't realise you're playing or have considered the following:

Who are the players?
You will never know all of them, and new ones are entering. But you need to get in there and know at least that they exist. Some players are not active, and others may be very soon. Social networks are a huge help on this. Browse your online contacts from time to time and you will find who changed jobs and where to.

We once bidded on a major design and build package with another partner company and we knew first hand that we were better positioned than the other competitor to win it. Surprisingly we got a phone call that neither had won and someone else did. Who? How did this happen, I wondered in shock? When I knew it was a relatively unknown smaller company under pricing us to get it, it struck me that players come and go all the time, and we were caught in the middle of this.

What are the rules?
Good question isn't it? The vast majority are unwritten, and the written ones (e.g. RFP) can possibly be "flexed". So don't take it so badly when you see them changing or don't like them

The first time I was asked to get a deadline extension I was shivering. That just did not seem right and nobody likes to "beg", but you may find yourself in this position and need to call or email someone with the arguments why it should be allowed. Sometimes you will get it and the buyer is normally used to people asking for it, so don't sweat too much about it. BUT prepare a plan B in case you don't!

What does the playing field look like?
Or in other words, what's your perception of the players and rules? Is it a fair all out on competitive products and pricing? Or is there something tilting it towards you or the competitors, such as national quotas? Don't assume it is all set in stone, because it's not!

What are the prizes and rewards?
If you're playing at something, you're looking for a reward. Is it reputation, market share, bonus?

Do your homework

How obvious and common sense and yet so overlooked. This is not just for meeting new people but with ANY current contacts, project meetings and virtually everything that you wish to make a visible contribution. Unless you want to be off the radar and be a wallflower, then don't.

BUT if you do want to be a player, do homework. It doesn't have to be a week's worth of work. Read the magazines about the highlights that may affect them. Quickly browse their webpage. Mention you are visiting X in a conversation with someone in common to see what their opinion is.

Reference it with dates

Referencing all your work, proposals and meeting notes with dates is one of the best little tricks in being an organized salesman. There is nothing worse than not being able to locate an important presentation, a proposal or a memo because you simply cannot remember where it's archived.

There is nothing more embarrassing trying to find in your million files and emails something you need to retrieve quickly while a client or a partner is waiting for you to move on. Sometimes you need to get something out quickly while the topic is hot and if you don't, the opportunity is gone. So better get organised as good as you can, or you'll eventually regret it.

Sell only when ready

Being proactive also has its drawbacks. I have repeatedly made this mistake. In the goodwill and keen ways of advancing initiatives, I have tried to sell new stuff to my client's or bosses without properly thinking it through. With some intelligent questioning your aspirations will fade away quickly if you have not prepared it (see also homework).

At a point in time, I wanted to hire someone, as I generally felt quite a lot of stuff was on my desk and could use a hand. Maybe a trainee would do.

So you go to your boss and tell him this. You don't tell him what tasks. You didn't really think how it may fit with current employment climate. You just feel like getting a hand. That was a bad idea. Boss says thinks about it and you get nothing in the end...

This is a lesson for selling something as trivial as that, even if you're doing it on your feet. Now extrapolate to the really important stuff.

Being ready means practicing. Like many competitive sports, you must practice enough a presentation or the topic until you feel "I'm ready, bring it on!"

This happened at a very high profile presentation. I knew it was a once in a lifetime shot to present at this conference and wanted to do it perfect, no more no less. For days I practiced over and over but even if I was satisfied with the contents I still wasn't totally happy with the delivery style. So what did I do? Practice and bore yourself until your gut says you're in shape. And only then I had a good night sleep and aced it the next day.

BC instead of BS

That's business case instead of bullshit for those who haven't figured it out yet. Everything has a reason to be or to move forward (or backwards, sideways or whatever the client wants). Give them what they want, not what you desire!

It's known than business cases normally tell you want you want to hear (if you're into entrepreneurship and business plan writing, you'll know what I mean). That's would be ok, if you're into tricking others or deceiving yourself.

I will always listen to a good reasoning and structured ideas or a business case. It makes me nervous when people tell me random stuff without a clear end point. You should think everything is a business case.

Why do it? What it entails? What's in it for me, you or the guy sitting next door?

Selling without thinking why the client needs it or how it may fit with their needs only takes you to the situation of the keen and enlightened engineer that pours out the supremacy of their products.

I once agreed to meet with a guy, who supposedly was a salesperson. He was, of course, an engineer full of high hopes for his product. It also happened that on that particular day I was short on time and we had to rush through the presentation. As he starts telling me all about the hardware, the capabilities, etc, I am sure my face changed into "why are you telling me this"? I work in an industry full of jargon, but this guy was from an electronics company, so that's more or less another universe for me! I was clueless about what I was supposed to do with that information and tried to redirect the conversation as to what we could do together. I don't remember hearing a consistent answer... he was just looking to download his product sheets onto my head and see if he was lucky...NOT!

I used to do this simple mistake quite often. Amazed by the technical superiority of our products and services, you lay out your references, expertise, clients and major achievements and expect the potential client to make sense out of it and employ you. WRONG!

These ONLY serve as background to your proposal. At some occasions it may not even be necessary to spell them out. You may at times know where you can help or solve the problem, and some other times not really.

In any case, you need to find something you can objectively accomplish for the client. Otherwise my friend, the chances are really slim

Think on your feet/improvise

This relates to proposals. You may be well prepared and have done your homework BUT you are late. Competitors are already there, the client is looking at something else, and his interests are not what you imagined.

I once went to see a potential customer to have a first contact and describe what my division could do with them. It turns out they were not so interested in this but in other services of our company. So imagine I had only one speech and could not detect these interests and improvise?

I ended up selling the other divisions and how they could help. In the end of the day, one should always remember you work for a company and you want to see it do well globally, not just your own, or otherwise your reputation for a self interested sales manager will come back to haunt you soon.

So you are ready, BUT you may need to improvise. This is why you think on your feet and re-focus what you can do instead.

Brief and to the point

Nobody has ever complained that a presentation is too short. If you start by respecting someone's time and being able to deliver a consistent and to the point pitch you will be very much appreciated.

At a session of organised B2B meetings, I once met with a procurement director. I am sure that after listening to half dozen regurgitated presentations he was not quite in the mood for yet another surprisingly technical superiority declaration. So his face and body language were obvious demonstrations of his state of mind.
As I declared it would be brief and to the point from the first minute, and actually keeping my promise (we used up 15 of the 30 minutes available), his mood changed and I think he captured my key messages.

A reflection of this is also when you start off with the corporate presentation of mission/vision/history of the company and founders, etc. RESIST doing this. The client, as you are also from time to time, while it may find mildly interesting, it's not what he's there to listen and to be quite blunt, irrelevant to his purposes. So skip it altogether, resume it in 10 seconds or you'll be starting off with the wrong foot.

Never underestimate

Lacking the use of a crystal ball, estimating is never easy, whether it is in the economic sense or guessing what will happen next or even more difficult, how someone or an adversary will react.

Some people argue you should not be estimating or thinking through scenarios as it's a waste of time because you will be always, to a certain extent, off the target. But what you cannot afford it is to NOT have a critical view or "guesstimate" certain aspects of a sales proposal. Stupid as it may seem, look at the unexpected as a possibility, no matter how wild it may seem. As I've learned the hard way, it can happen...

We once bidded on a very important and large work package against a very well known consulting firm. The initial estimate was that they were going to be more expensive than us and to ensure we would not lose it; we priced aggressively and thought it was nearly there. After not winning the bid, we later found out that the competitor did the unexpected and underpriced us heavily thus kicking us out in a way we would never foresee!

Never enough data

(Depeche Mode – I just can't get enough)

This is the eternal dilemma between salespeople and engineers supporting a presentation or a bid. There is never enough data. Never!

The tendency is to request having so much detail that you nearly deliver the final solution. People sometimes forget it's a PROPOSAL! You are proposing to do something, not actually do it right now! That's later and it's called a project!

OK, you do need some information to calculate the resources dedication, travel costs, and plenty of other small things, especially if you're manufacturing something.

What baffles the average engineer (and remember I am one) is that step away from the comfort zone and into the conceptual sales pitch. You may need to guesstimate what the customer needs. You may of course, be wrong about it, but hey you got to give it a go. This trial and error search and persistence for that sale is not really understood among most of the engineering crowd.

I am not picking on them, and just as an example that you may need to use what you have and get on with it. There are never the perfect conditions or the ideal set of data, and you may need to settle for something less than good, but you cannot afford to work for months on getting an RFP and then declare foul (meaning, missing data, unclear requirements, incoherent product structure, and the list can go on and on) from the customer's side. You can, and should ask if it's reasonable, if you do not genuinely understand a document received or, ask for a deadline extension. More about this one later on...

Mock up

In the same way others go to market first with prototypes and mockups, you too should think of doing so when rolling out a new prouduct or service, in the sense of how you intend to sell it.

What you want to avoid is the typical "I don't get it" or that people miss the point, especially if you only have one shot to deliver your pitch!

Why not write it down and practice with others in your office, or try it with a relative or someone out of your context. If they understand what you're on about, surely you will face better odds to be sucessful with others!

Follow up

Most people just don't follow up and therefore are not persistent enough. If there was anything I've learned was to be persistent and follow up. I cannot overemphasize this. If you can't follow up, you can't sell. And following up is not just asking if someone read your email. It's about being creative, looking to transmit subtle messages and finding more opportunities to pitch your products and services.

3 strikes and you're out

(Daft Punk – One more time)

As a customer, who I am from time to time, I am always amazed by the lack of persistence from the salesman at hand, without being inconvenient of course (see also 3Ps).

I hear from fellow colleagues "I sent him an email, but he didn't reply". This can go on for weeks or months, until you lose momentum or faith that something will happen (secretly wishing that this person will read it and come back to you full of business opportunities).

Well, guess again.

I use the "3 strikes and you're out rule". When I mean "out" does not mean I give up. It just tells me to have a fresh look or another strategy to start again.

Normally a first email contact should be brief and ask for an action/reply. Sometimes people haven't had the time to read or reply, or have forwarded to someone else. This happens very often.

So set yourself a reasonable period of time to follow up. If you think one week is good enough, add a task to your list and come back then.

If you don't get an answer, forward your original email so that people don't have to go looking for what you sent before.

Repeat for a third time, but change your email preceding the old text! How stupid or lazy (or both) you will look if you just forward an email with no text!

Statistics:
- First time email contacts very often have to be followed up.
- Second time follow up has most replies.
- Third time emails are for tough cases, but works. People will eventually be a bit embarrassed for not replying to the previous two and will do something about it.

If this still doesn't work, and using the phone is an option, USE IT!

Even if I know this from experience, I was astonished when I was presenting to a potential customer what we could do together, and this guy in particular I had chased him for 4 months, so I wasn't too sure if I had crossed the line of being too pushy, but there I was. When I timidly apologised for hopefully not being a pain, he says in a very relaxed way that he did not expect anything else from a person in my job. I wish every potential client was as understanding as this one...but then again I know that from now onwards I need to ask him repeatedly!

Have a follow up list

(Gwen Stefani-what are you waiting for?)

As you start having to manage multiple opportunities, you will quickly find yourself with an urge to remember who you have contacted, when is the next time you should contact them and whatever relevant info you may deem adequate. In other words, you need a mini CRM.

While I am not against those expensive software packages, I find it that keeping it simple is more than enough. I mean, all you need to follow up is a list of who, when and a piece of relevant information. Do you really need to know all the corporate stats, phone and fax numbers, and exact time of your last calls? Sure, have an updated address book and some sort of portfolio of info. But for day to day follow up keep it REALLY simple.

I've made it work for me in my own way. It's also great for internal communications so that people see what the progress, no matter how painful and slow, is happening in a structured way.

Fwd!

One common and unconscious mistake with following up email communications is sending a simple note such as *"Have you read or considered what I sent you two weeks ago?"*

This is gold to an overworked colleague/customer. Make them find an old email in their thousands of emails for no good reason (at least they don't know one, if you haven't told them!)

Save them the hassle (and why should they bother anyway!), and increase your probabilities of a decent reply. Forward the previous email so that they can scroll down straight away and refresh their clouded memories of a possibly vague and rambling email.

Follow the trail

(The Smiths – How soon is now)

Never soon enough to start following the trail.

You may start off a bit naive and think you have found THE person that is exactly positioned at the potential client to make your pitch or give you that opportunity.

Here's more discouraging news. You may find yourself in a tunnel of forwarding emails and referrals that will burn out your patience.

Sometimes the guy at question is "too high" in the organization, meaning he does not get his hands dirty in procuring. So he passes the ball to the procurement guys.

The procurement guy more often than not, will not budge if someone technical will not tell him what to buy and how at what price. It may be he does not know your organization, so why should he invite you? (Unless the top guy says so explicitly).

The average technical guy feels somewhat trapped when you talk to him/her. Why? He is in a "noble" job; he also does not want to get his hands dirty at negotiating and talking money and conditions.

Another situation is going cold call or by some social network asking for a phone call or an email address. You can be chasing 3-5 individuals in a row to get to...see beginning of this chapter. At this point most of the time you're flying half blind because you do not know how serious the other people are (NOTE: this has changed a lot, making contacts on professional networking sites is no longer seen as something useless).

Perhaps this is the most frustrating part of any sales campaign. It happened to me having to insist with someone for some months and then be informed he left the company, and nearly having to start all over again. I had to backtrack to another contact and ask who to contact. That led me to another person that took my request and also moved on!! And then again to another person which passed on the ball to someone else.

If you persist and follow the trail eventually you will be in contact with someone that is willing to listen to you. Then it's the time to not waste that opportunity

Pick up the vibes

You need to be attuned to the "vibes" you get when contacting someone. Resonating is very important.

If in the middle of some conversation a potential client says *"I can never find time to meet people in the morning as I am so busy, I tend to book my meetings at the late part of the day"*. This says tonnes. Don't call her in the morning to have a chat. Respect her busy and productive time.

Other type of vibes may be with relation to other companies, or just by chit chat you find something in common. Just ready any book about emotional intelligence and you will know what I mean.

People in your business or industry are always curious about who is doing what, and if they are nice guys or not. See also later on about reputations. You can have a picture of yourself, but it's not you that sends the "vibes" around, it's the others.

Send thank you notes

It doesn't matter whether you use email or a hand written note. Be sure that after each visit or new contact to send a thank you note or a pleased to meet you. It refreshes people's memory and reinforces the connection.

If you're using a social network like Linkedin, make sure to send a thanks note to someone accepting your invite. I can tell you that those that have sent me a little thanks email for sure are far more visible or easily remembered than everybody else, even if I have no idea or immediate business need with them.

Write a template if you just want to copy and paste, in several languages if you want it to be really professional. People appreciate the time to say thanks and look forward to do business or hearing back from those that remembered them. It's just plain human nature at play

Use read receipts

I use it always. Not that I am paranoid about it, and it doesn't always works as some people decline sending them. Most people don't know it they have it in automatic.

Use it when you have met someone and have sent him a thank you note, or let's follow up, or some materials. It's good for the "3 strikes and out" to get your head counting.

You may also from time to time have the unpleasant surprise people deleted it without even reading it. This is a pretty good hint that your strategy may not be quite right in the approach, or occasionally that this person forwarded to someone and deleted (you do not have the luxury of knowing this in 99% of the times). At this time you should also think about not giving up and resetting your mind to this particular target

Or a receipt 6 months after you've sent it also says a lot about the other person. One thing you DO NOT do is call someone saying I KNOW you deleted my email. It's perhaps the worse remedy and unless it's a matter of life and death, you must resist the temptation of picking up the phone or sending another one mentioning you know about what he's done with your email.

The phone

Email can be so easy to use that you may forget you actually need to speak to people.

As it is widely known, email is the least effective means of communication, because you cannot transmit "tone of voice" and no body language. "Tone of voice" is useful because others can pick up if you're being sarcastic or joking, and with email missing that component. It's something that probably leads to those many rebounded emails with out of tone replies. Body language in many cases you're better off not having it, if you're the kind that let's emotions take over and trust me, some people will see through you.

Body language of others in situations where you need to assess how things are doing is to your advantage and this is why it's much better to have face to face contact to assess whether you're on the right track.

So the phone is a good option if you want to avoid email misunderstandings and cannot afford for some reason the chance for face time. So you cannot live without it.

The tough part is using it well. Email is easy because you can take your time to write a draft, review it, save it to send later on and even delete it if you're not sure about what you want to communicate.

But the phone can be much more intimidating. An unplanned call may be more damaging than 50 emails, if you just make up something on the spot, or don't feel comfortable with your sales pitch. Personally it's a tool that should be used more frequently, rather than the email. I guess a lot of people prefer to lose out on the "tone of voice" feedback in favour of having "proof" of what they meant. I am sure you too have done at some time, to have it in writing rather than calling someone. Or in the reverse situation, it's better to verbally disclose something than to write it, as you never know where emails will end up.

You also need to manage the convenience of making or picking up a call. These are two very different situations.

Never make a phone call when there is bad network coverage, too much noise or in a place where you should not be. Think about what you want to say and what you expect of the call. Do you know if this person will be the type of a few minutes straight to the point or is he/she more of a chatterbox? Do they like to have "preliminary" chit chat about sports and families, or are they just to the point?

About picking up a call, you should also measure the convenience of doing it. If your mobile phone is up to date and synchronised with your email server contacts list you should have no problem identifying a caller. Those that don't, well you need to take your chances, but don't get paranoid about not taking any either. It helps if your voicemail is active so you don't lose any calls.

Another thing to remember about some phone calls or emails; they are like a silver bullet, you have only one shot at it. When you know someone at very high level that you can call or owes you a favour, sometimes it's like a silver bullet. There will not be a second chance; in fact you may be lucky if there is a first chance!

Don't stand in line

(Gun – Stand in line)

Don't wait until someone calls you. Or if you know the competition is closing in on a deal, jump the line and call the purchaser and ask for a new opportunity.

Moreover, don't wait for things to happen. It's ok to set yourself some time to follow up, but waiting for the sake of expecting for the best outcome without taking action is just nonsense. But choose wisely jumping the line. If the customer or the generally accepted rules go against that, it could get you into more trouble than benefit.

5 why's

(Moby – Why does my heart feel so bad?)

You may know this from the Lean techniques. When something doesn't work, ask 5 times why it is like that to ensure you are thinking about all alternatives. There will be times that you may not see "the light at the end of the tunnel" or something smells fishy. Make an effort to think hard and ask yourself repeatedly why it's like this (or if it's too late, what the hell happened!)

This is also related to the rules of the game. It may be you thought you understood the dynamics and who the players were, but you need to repeatedly ask why, why, why!

We once lost an important deal after being in the lead and getting all the hints from the customer that we we're poised to win it. We didn't. Something happened, so why, why, why?

I later found out that there were links between the customer top management and the competition that tilted their way. If I knew this in advance, would I have acted differently? Probably not, as it was clearly out of my control. But at least expectations were different inside my organisation and we would have invested less time in dealing with the bid.

Do it yourself

When it comes to follow up, delegate as little as possible. This may sound going against all expert advice on people and time management, but think again. It's all well and good to get someone in your team doing that sort of work, but be very picky. You may delegate and then regret it, especially in this sort of delicate theme.

A guy in my office was running a project and we were hoping for a big scope extension. This guy is not commercially focused, but given he was in contact for the current project work, it sounded like a good idea to let him poke the client for the "what next".
He ended up involving other people that we're not supposed to, resulting in an internal block and hampering the direct line of communication. It wasn't his fault, but I should have known better than to do it like that, so never again. Next time I will do it myself, it's worth the effort.

Tell people what you're up to

It's not just important to be good at what you do, but equally to LOOK good. This means communicating your progress and successes to a wide number of audiences. While you do that, don't exaggerate or scale down. Be honest and humble. Many people in a normal conversation will quickly pick up whether you're into "hard sell" or having a pleasant chat about what's going on. Many times people will offer to help and will most definitely echo your company's track record and latest news without being asked. How many times have you heard through the grapevine "Hey, did you hear these guys just got a contract with XYZ"?

Biz cards for what?

(Faith No More- Introduce yourself)

It does not matter how many big shots or business card you have if you have nothing to sell that interest them. I've seen fellow salespeople quite proud of their stack of business cards, yet not having anything interesting or of interest to this people. This is OK if and only if you can network with them to pursue other avenues and referrals; otherwise those are not worth chasing yet.

Remember to always keep them as people change jobs and things evolve all the time.

Positivity

If you have never received an email wih dubious intentions or conflictive text, then you haven't seen anything. Your first reaction will be to shoot from the hip a reply line by line an argument by argument.

A good way to blow steam is to start any conversation, phone call or email stating something positive. This helps the receiver to be more receptive to whatever you want to say next, BUT this does not mean that once you say something positive (not to be confused with something nice and useless), you can say whatever you want.

The point is to start with a good foot and state of mind to then say or debate the points at hand. With time it brings benefits, first of all you will be less prone to writing stuff that could get you in trouble or worsen a situation, and put yourself in a mentally positive state to be more productive. Easy stuff isn't it?

Relationships

As long as we are dealing with people and not machine interfaces, relationships are key and central to the process of selling. We are caught in an infusion of networks and ways of doing business. Never email has had such importance, and social networks becoming centrepiece for business development. What this means for the sales process is that things are not clear cut. You will meet so many more people than you ever thought, in person and virtually, and your resources available and expert advice are many times more than anyone would foresee 10 years ago.

Who's on your side?

(Rage against the machine – Know your enemy!)

Easy question isn't it? As you go in to more complex sales processes that involve multiple stakeholders, you will soon be asking who is on your side.

A particular client we later found out that he was more interested in showing no one could do the job, so that he could keep it in house. We went through several stages of bidding and got to the point where we met all the required criteria and delivered rigorously all the documentation, so we were sure winners. Ah...not yet. I was shocked to hear it was going to start all over due to lack of competitors (say WHAT?), even if we managed 3 stages of bidding.

On your side does not mean not against you. It may very well be someone influential but neutral. You would expect customers to play the game in a neutral way to get the best proposals, wouldn't you?

And you are not on your own. Sometimes going in a new direction with a new project may affect internally the org structure, and you may not get the support you hoped for from some internal department. Would you be surprised if what you're trying to sell impacts the way of working?

Stay in touch

When I was starting in my business development role, I was immersed in contacting pretty much everyone I knew from my business cards collection. I could not think of a better way to start developing the business in the absence of any major directions or training received. I also worked for an organization where there was nearly no dedicated business development and nearly everything was still to be done.

In one of those occasions, one person told me, "hey don't worry I understand sales people need to be in contact". Never until then had it dawned on me so clear (although instinctively it was) that staying in contact is the key and most people will be OK with that (as long as you're not a pain in the back side).

While I am not the king at doing this (like sending short notes on everybody's birthdays and special occasions), I felt the need to feel well and not let someone important (in the sense of important to me as relationship) to go uncontacted for too long.

The simplest of strategies is to send a thanks email after a new contact or meeting. Take 1 minute and the other person will reinforce their memory of you. Even better, summarize the output of the meeting and propose help or deliver whatever you agreed to do.

Keeping in touch can also mean using the "3 strikes and out" approach.

It's all about relationships

(Queen – It's a kind of magic)

Maintaining and nurturing good relationships with people you have good empathy will always pay off with time. If they are true friends then the pay off question is not even there.

If you have made an effort in some way to develop a new contact with opening possibilities for him or her, you can be sure that next time he has something on his desk that could be of interest will call you.

It's the age old first give then you can take. But you must give.

We once had to put together a consortium of companies, so I had to cold call one of them and scan their interest in joining. A year later after we worked together and knew each other better, this guy asked me why and how I managed to track him down. When I said about knowing his company reputation and just calling the receptionist and asking to talk to him, you could see the look of surprise on his face. Anyway, he was so happy that I did so that, when he had some business opportunities suited to our expertise, he just called us and no one else.

How long is your address book?

(Metallica – Holier than you)

"It's not who you are, it's who you know"
Mock as much as you want as a disbeliever of social networks, but if you still think you already know enough people, you're just wrong, sorry to be the bearer of bad news.

A senior guy once told me that the value of some people, even if they are worthless workers, is the extent of their network and contacts list. While knowing people does not guarantee success, having a wide range of contacts sure helps. And your perceived value in the organisation will be more than you can estimate right now.

A word of warning about the breadth and spread of contacts. It is useless to claim 5000 contacts if they're all open networkers with no interest to you, unless you're just playing the odds of something accidentally happening.
In general your network should have some people with mutual interests, no matter how obvious this may seem it turns out to be a strategy. Have a spread of industries (centre your attention on yours of course), functions, disciplines and for personal interest, recruiters and head hunters, journalists and other walks of life that may at some point in time need to contact for some reason.

There is also a great evolution from people realising networking is not just with people you have actually met (this is the other narrow extreme vs. all out open networkers). It's normal and acceptable to add people you haven't (yet perhaps) or never will meet during your lifetime. However they may know something or need something from you and vice versa.

And... Just when you thought you had the perfect contact (finally!) at a potential client, the guy leaves. Unless you have managed to know more people inside the organization, such as his boss, or other subordinates that might take up the position, if you're aiming for a single point of contact, the odds are that with time it will fade away.
You simply cannot rely on just knowing one "head honcho". Then again don't go crazy trying to get to know absolutely everybody in a certain organisation.

You may have developed for some time a contact with the technical guy, which is sympathetic with your pitch for the services you can provide. As it happens in many cases, he may not really want or can push forward the possibility of accepting a proposal.

You can then, if you have the contact, with diplomacy and care, go to the next level and talk to his boss. This is great, because now the technical guy can openly say to his boss how good he feels about you, but the danger lies if his boss is not convinced. This means you cannot go back to the technical guy and start again, and he is very likely not going to go against his direct superior. So the higher in the organization you pitch the higher the stakes of all or nothing.

It's a small world. Really. You should accept it like it is, and face the consequences that everybody knows everybody, especially in some industries or sectors. I don't mean by having physically met, but knowing of someone's existence or reputation.

Reputations, hard to build and easy to destroy

(Bon Jovi – Dead or alive)

In the commercial world reputations are an asset. A reputation can open or close doors, and I don't mean just your company, but your own. In fact there will be times people will pick the phone because it's YOU. Because YOU have developed a reputation for working hard, negotiating well or something else you have accomplished that people respect and did not forget.

Having a reputation, a good one of course, is hard work day in and day out. It is a consequence of many things, such as doing your job well, developing and maintaining good relationships and getting along well with (most) people.

Reputations (or sometimes confused with perceptions) are very volatile. I can't claim to have the best reputation with all people, but I do have an honest feel (even if I am wrong sometimes) of how people see me.

I have also experienced how your company's reputation may slant how people relate with you in first instance. You work for a large multinational? You're a god of engineering, you have the best product and you're smart as hell.

If you work for another underdog company, you will spend most of your time selling who they are and what they do, and building the reputation from scratch (centrepiece in business development).

The volatility is perhaps the scariest part. You may work for months getting things on its path and getting known to deliver. And one day you may screw up, something went out of control and next thing you know there are no amount of apologies that can put your reputation back on its track.

It is very hard to accept this if you work hard at building and maintaining a profile. When you blow steam it may affect it, but I am still adamant that there are things one should not put up with. But balance your act and bite your tongue if you have to. It sucks but it comes with the job.

Friendships

(Queen –friends will be friends)

I had a teacher at the MBA that was not one of the most pleasant ones. Not that he was offensive or anything like that, it's just that he did not engage in small talk before classes or smiled a lot. He seemed in many ways a type of "harsh but fair" kind of bloke. What I remember most from his lectures is not what he had to say about balanced scorecards, but a sort of philosophy lesson about friendship.

Many MBA classes are filled with young and confident professionals, some assertive, some arrogant as hell, and some even malicious (you get to see this at group work), given it's an all out competition not to be in the back end of the Gauss curve. This means that you want to get along with your colleagues but deep down everybody is anxious to see who falls first (in "real life" somehow it's not exactly the same).

So his view was that we should be there to learn and enjoy our time, not necessarily to be friends with everybody. He did not mean not being friendly with people; it's just that it's impossible to be friends with everybody around you.

At first this shocked me for the clean and crystal clear way he poured this knowledge onto the class. At that point I implicitly had a rule of always wanting to get along and be friends with as many people as I could (I still hold this motto deep inside), but the fact is that it is not easy once you get stepped on by some jerk wanting to be on the top of the class.

As time passes you will meet many many more people and make peace that you can be cordial but not necessarily friends with the whole wide world. In fact there are times that for whatever reason you specifically will not want to be friends with someone.

A good story (not claimed as mine and more as a joke) that illustrates how friendship can be is about the little bird that was flying south for the winter. "It was so cold that the bird froze and fell to the ground in a large field. While it was lying there, a cow came by and dropped some dung on it. As the frozen bird lay there in the pile of cow dung, it began to realise how warm it was. The dung was actually thawing him out! He lay there all warm and happy, and soon began to sing for joy. A passing cat heard the bird singing and came to investigate.
Following the sound, the cat discovered the bird under the pile of cow dung, and promptly dug him out and ate him!

1) Not everyone who drops shit on you is your enemy.

2) Not everyone who gets you out of shit is your friend.

3) And when you're in deep shit, keep your mouth shut"

That says it all about friends and enemies! Next time there's some crap coming your way, remember these three lines and you will have a better view of the world!

Evangelize the boss

Sometimes no matter how good the boss is, he will not admit to a crude reality right away or take a decision on the spot. That's mostly because they have the experience of controlling the impulse of deciding something right away or because he simply did not come to terms with the impact of the message being received.

So you need to say it as many times as many it may require to get things going. If you truly believe it's worth pursuing, get your arguments and ideas together and educate your boss (yes, he also can learn something more, not just you!)

Evangelists, as they are in fashion today, are just persistent people.

And if you are persistent with all your potential customers, why should you not do the same with your internal customer?

Never dis(card)

You may be tempted to throw away those old business cards, whether because you think that person will probably have forgotten you or will not respond, or it may be that he or she has moved on.

That's a mistake! Every business card should be kept religiously. You never know when you need to come back to this person, if circumstances change or to update your network when YOU move on.

After two years of no contact with one particular engineering director of a company which at first did not seem attractive to us, I decided to take a chance and insist on a meeting. I was pleasantly surprised to see him answer within 15 minutes confirming his interest in a meeting. As soon as this happened, I fired up the word processor and wrote this. It struck me so hard I started doing the same for others in my collection of business cards. Funny enough I got some good replies and if nothing else, refreshed my connection with these persons.

Learning to say no is hard

Saying no to something is hard, because if you're focused on creating a good relationship you don't want things to go sour or people to think you're acting negative. But as I've learned the hard way, saying no requires serious assertiveness and it may save you a lot of hassle later on.

A client once recommended a person for a vacant position we were covering. Although this person seemed straight away a strong superstar, with a little investigation we found out we could not afford that hiring.
At a later stage we were asked how the hiring of that person was progressing. At this point we should have said: "Listen, we made some thorough analysis and we cannot afford to hire this excellent candidate, sorry". And that would probably be fine.
Instead, with the best of intentions we called the candidate to offer something below its known expectations, which of course led to nowhere.
So not only we wasted our time with something that could never work, but we also created false expectations with the client that there was a possibility we could hire that person he recommended.

Sales and technical people are different

(Kenny Loggins - Playing with the boys)

Depending on where you work a reputation will come with the job description. I am always amused when I remember a guy from my company assuming sales guys like me were always up to some no good schemes and negotiating everything that crossed our paths. He assumed we were different, and yes we were but not in the way he though we were. So admit there are differences and you must learn to deal with the lifeblood of engineering companies....

I once heard a conversation between two friends, both of them working in technical areas and talking about promoting a meeting. One of them needed access to the others site and the other one said if we can get a genuine reason to schedule one it would be easier. Remember these guys just want to get together to talk technical stuff but can't escape their day job responsibilities. I was quite amused with this as any half decent sales guy would just make up an excuse to make the meeting happen! How obvious! So when I suggested to my friends this possibility, they were laughing but I think deep down they were still sceptical. The thing is while others may see you as not being focused and wanting a distraction (sales has a reputation for long lunches and golf courses), for the savvy sales guy is another opportunity to make it happen and do networking.

Not everything you do is directly productive or can be logically justified. Engineers find this hard to accept in their orderly life.

At times spending money going to some event where there is no sight of the return on money spent does not mean it is not worthwhile pursuing. This may sound like black arts but it is actually feeling the terrain and looking to new avenues.

Einstein said it's the things that matter most that are harder to measure and vice versa. Now that's some powerful stuff from a technical guy that every salesman should remember. So for important things be wary of too many performance indicators!

Job titles

In any business job titles are ALWAYS something people pay attention. If you are doing online networking, are you not more easily attracted to click on the profile of a CEO, "head of", or VP, instead of someone with "senior engineer" or "seeking a new challenge"?

Job titles can also be misleading, and some peopple use that to their own advantage on purpose. It's easier to get people's attention if you have a title like director or VP.

Remember we are in the business of knowing people and selling. What this means is that while you, like many others, will be attracted to interesting job titles, what I've learned the hard way is that they do not mean competence or humanity, two basic qualities on decision makers.

Some of these people enter a state of "busyness" (see chapter on this later on) that they genuinely feel they MUST be busy and unavailable. People that do this are also 99% of the times not very competent at what they are doing, and this mean that you must take it into account when you are following up or communicating with them.

Very quickly you will pick up those that have big job titles and are not responding to emails and need to consistently be chased, or those that are good business people and understand both where they are and where you sit and do.

Make it happen

So you know who's interested and has some money to spend, now what? It's not self evident that your products and services and the client's needs are a perfect match, so now it's time to tighten the nuts!

Ask for action

This is a lesson learned that as obvious as it may seem (also known in various presentation courses as "call to action"), it's something people do not normally incorporate in their daily tasks.

Here's a little story to show that *Casanova was a salesman!*
A young man, knowing Casanova was in his final moments, asked to see him urgently in the hope he would reveal his secret for being so successful with women.

As he approaches Casanova in his dying breath, he is told to come close so that he could whisper that magnificent secret that made him famous with the female gender.

As the young man listens attentively, Casanova says "so you really want to know my secret?" The young man nods in anxiety for the big revelation.

Casanova then simply says "I asked"

Here's a lesson for all salespeople, what you don't ask you don't get. Just like Casanova did.

Especially in the engineering community, they are so convinced of the benefits and advantages of their product or service that they believe (we really do!), that by just giving information to potential customers a light bulb will come on and straight away a flurry of requests and contracts will flow.

Forget it. First of all, most people, and the higher in any organization, rarely read a full email or open attachments, much less take the time to reflect and reply with what next.

Second, even if you're lucky, don't make them think. YOU are the one that should know what you want from them! If you don't know this when you contact a potential customer, stop right now. Take a break, have a cup of coffee and find inspiration and be ready for perspiration.

You may want different things from different people. A conference call to break first ground, a face to face to advance something already started.

If you from first moment have an idea of WHAT you want or wish to propose, do it! The odds are that customers will see that you are a focused and objective oriented guy that will not waste his or her precious time. If it's a no-go, at least they now know you and that you are REALLY proactive.

BUT be careful if you think asking is just a procedure. It's an opportunity not to be missed and must be done well, as opposed to mindlessly bombarding people with requests. Be elaborate, to the point and polite at all times. If someone says no, take it graciously and decide carefully what next.

Again back to the technical superiority syndrome or feeling that there is no competition (or they're sleeping on the job). No matter how good your products or services are, the world is spinning regardless and people are doing what they need to do. They are not waiting for you to come and rescue or enlighten them. Forget about that. If you get the opportunity to go and talk to an established company this is a fact you should accept, the sooner the better.

Don't push people on stage

(Therapy – Nowhere)

If you push people on stage, I'll tell you where you will end up. Nowhere.

Presentations can be a one time shot and in itself are a world full of advices of do and don'ts.

Here's one don't. Don't put a non sales oriented person to talk/ramble about previous projects technical characteristics, when he is not a good presenter, has difficulties in expressing fluently in another language, and what's worse, he did not practice the presentation.

This level of improvisation and risk taking is a killer. Or a near death experience.

We once went to see a top guy in large company that was a prime potential client, which after 3 months of asking for an opportunity to present our services and references finally agreed. So far so good.

Take the standard corporate presentation and some slides about previous projects. Ok too! Except I was still acting like the engineer proud of the technical superiority of its products and services.

Then with all the good intentions present your part and pass it on to the technical guy. Remember, he is not an ace at presenting, not comfortable with another language and really did not dedicate any time to the presentation.

It was a Catastrophe. He rambled in too much detail, forward and backwards with the slides, improvising and choking.
The potential client must have thought what the hell was going on.

Conclusion: Do not risk a good presentation and opportunity if you are not sure the person or team can't deliver in a half decent way. Leave him/her/them at home if you have too, you're better off.

Sell it...even if it's free!

Amazingly even if you offer something for free you have to sell it!

I once took the initiative for potential customers, for long term strategic reasons, propose to do small projects for free to gain their trust and show how good we were. We went one step further and identified some projects that were, in our opinion, improvements needed sooner or later and how we could deliver something useful for that company and not just an academic exercise.

With one company we identified three projects at a visit. We wrote down how and why we should to them. We waited a couple of months. Then we found out they were already doing two of them. Honestly they did them without our hints as we did not follow up enough on the proposals.

Well, after some twists and turns, we got to a point where the project was clearly identified, what was the problem, scope of work, etc.

All stars lined up. We were going to solve or help to improve a known issue, deliver benefits and do it for free. From their side there were no resources, other than those that needed to be interviewed occasionally and with little real work to do.

Guess what? The receiving director was totally convinced on doing it. FANTASTIC. Yeah...but he still needed to SELL it to his VP. And he, the director, is not a salesman. So I was asked to help him out with selling it.

Now you see what I mean with selling even if it's free.

The good news is that it's a great opportunity to help and impress the future client, practice your sales skills and develop the relationship. So don't get pissed off with having to sell your self evident benefits but make the best of it.

Are you excited enough not to sleep?

(I'm so excited – The Pointer Sisters)

During a period of time while I was managing a students association, me and another colleague were so excited with what we were doing that many times while I was trying to sleep, new ideas would come to my mind and I would jump out of bed to write them in a piece of paper, and in many occasions stay for a while working on it. We would often call each other at incredible hours like 4:30 AM just to ask for each other's opinions and what next. This was quite normal and no one would complain at whatever ridiculous times we would call.

That often reminds me the level of excitement and commitment one has to have to skip sleeping and be always on for whenever someone wants to talk about business with you.

Don't draw the wrong conclusions. I am not suggesting not sleeping or being constantly excited. But if it doesn't make your heart beat faster when something happens you've been working on for months goes well, either you're in the wrong job or you're a lizzard!

Selling sand in the desert

Most salespeople envy those that have a product or service that sells on its own, whether it's because of brand name, reputation or any other characteristic. Don't envy them, if they don't have to make an effort, they're not much of a salesman are they? If you're like the vast majority that may not be selling Coca-Cola, you may feel at times like selling sand in desert, I mean a commodity in a crowded marketplace or in a sales setting very difficult to sell.

You should never give up or despair, as you cannot just make excuses that your product or service is no good, that the times are bad or that customers are too demanding or don't know what they want. You must find a way to sell your special sand.

As thin as ice

You may also find yourself in very "thin ice" when you have to engage potential customers that are hardly considering you, or for some reason you have a shot at pitching to them but knowing beforehand the chances are very unlikely. This does not mean giving up or not bothering. You should take every chance to pitch your products or services, consider it a training run, as long as you don't act like a practice presentation, which would really get you in trouble!

Sometimes it's just their built in protection to be careful with any new company. If you are honest and play your cards right, you will be surprised about how some of these initially tense and cold relationships turn out to be better than you expected.

Push if worth pushing

(Garbage – Push it)

You should never give up, but sometimes leave it when you can't get the internal push for some proposal or contribution. Then again you should measure in your mind about pushing if you truly believe it's worth pushing. There may not be many occasions, but trust me one will come and you will recognize it and regret you did not see it coming.

At a point in time I needed the support from another business development director. I worked hard at getting him on the map with a new client and after several weeks of silence I get a nice speech about not being attractive enough for him, due to many reasons. So I left it there and though he's the one to lose the opportunity, if he can't recognise a good one, his problem.

Well, at another meeting with the same potential client he states he was expecting some drawings or sketches for new facilities, in theory to be delivered by my uninterested colleague. That was right on my face with my managing director next to me wondering what went wrong and why was this potential client sort of upset of not seeing anything on the table...
The moral of the story: I should have anticipated the desire of the potential client for some sexy sketches and not dropped it with my colleague. We could have capitalized big time, instead we went away with a new homework list...

Don't ask

If you're not sure you will hear want you want to hear, then don't ask.
If you feel strongly about a line of action and have doubts whether your boss or colleague feels the same way, then take the route of executive decision and deal with his complaint later.
If you go the easy mushy feely way of asking him about something more or less trivial, he may off the cuff knock it down when you were burning to do it.

In this case, I wanted to make sure a potential client would see in writing the steps agreed at the meeting. Given it was a long conversation, the boss did not feel it was adequate to insist so much on the process, which I was instead very much in favour of doing so.

So what happened when I asked what he thought about sending this 3 bullet point process proposal? Nah, it's too formal, no need for that.
Not what I wanted to hear...Later on the momentum dropped below my expectations and I take it this happened because we did not dare writing down an agreed plan with the potential client.

The dating game

Going to certain events is like getting a date. You go and check out what's on the market and try to get a date to get to know them better. It's a fact that many people go to conferences and events, some not in their native language, and don't ask any questions to the presenter or make an effort to get to know the speakers and exchange business cards, especially Latin's like me tend to stick to the people they already know simply because it's the most comfortable thing to do. Well, that's just wrong and a waste of time.

Think of any event as going to a bar to meet ladies. You go there to get some action, not stand at the bar having a drink!

You
the Salesman

So you're into sales, so what? Very likely you are still someone's employee and the world is still revolving whether you do it better or worse than yesterday. Are you ready for a rollercoaster ride?

You have always been selling!

That's right you!
You had the sell your ideas, find cooperation from others, or as mundane as convincing (=selling) to your wife or girlfriend about going to see one movie instead of the other.
Most people HATE the word selling because of the negative connotations associated with wise guys trying to take your money or cheating you, and many more clichés and common perceptions.
BUT every time YOU have to convince someone, or want to get something, you are into selling mode. It may not be so elaborate or long term as you may find in other environments, but you are doing it and have done it for a long time!

Deadlines

Working in sales or business development inevitably revolves around deadlines. After all, your work is geared towards getting those opportunities to write proposals that will bring the business to your company, and naturally the customer will set deadlines for your replies.

One of the curious aspects of time in this context is that it can change unexpectedly. I mean, you can be asking for months what's going on and when will the RFP be released, and next thing you know you must deliver a proposal tomorrow morning, this afternoon if possible... So you can never really plan nor should you assume time is plenty, because it never is.

Writing proposals means working in a team of people, the more complex the bid the more interactions, chapters, requirements and checklists. So you must plan when you expect everybody's contributions in order for someone (you, of course) to integrate into a coherent document, review it, get it approved if it needs to and deliver to the customer. Now this may seem a milk run but it's actually much harder. Most contributors are NOT fully devoted to writing proposals and will be pulled in as required, and you have no direct oversight of their time so you need to be negotiating and asking about WIP constantly.

It may come to a point that, for some reason or another, you need a deadline extension. This is the most feared moment. You feel like a schoolboy that did not finish their homework and now needs to talk to the teacher about more time to finish the duties.

The first time my boss asked me to call a procurement guy to ask for an extension I was petrified. I was all fidgety and nervous because I could not really see how I was going to pull it off to allow us finishing our proposals. What would this guy say or think? How would he react to our lateness?

After picking up the phone and making up some arguments on why we needed more time to deliver a good proposal, the guy on the other side of the phone allowed the extension. Boy was I in a happy mood.

History repeats itself and time is never enough (see also the chapter about never enough data) and you end up asking for more extensions. Sometimes you will get it and some others no. But you still have to plan your way around it and get it out the door.

The hunter in you

(Metallica - Of wolf and man)

I love music and you always find interesting stuff in what you hear. Metallica's "Of Wolf and Man" spells out your salesman karma:
"I hunt therefore I am"
Salespeople are inherently hunters. They like to be out there smelling the terrain and hunting down opportunities. It's in their nature. You can of course, learn how to hunt, but you're better off if you're blood starts pumping when you think about going out there and doing your stuff.

You also need to refrain the instinct to be on the road 24/7 (at least on my industry). Just think of the office as a place to regroup your thoughts and get the resources and time off to think you need.

Until the fat lady sings...

When it's not over don't celebrate too soon. You may find yourself in a string of "leads" and "promises" and over communicating these will only, with time, make people think of you as over optimistic or not fulfilling those promises. Aim to strike a balance between communicating honestly and realistic expectations, and "tweeting" every email, phone call or gossip you encounter.

This is true at the beginning of any job. You want your boss to see you're making inroads, progressing and that things are happening. So every time you have a hot lead you ring him and tell him about how exciting this could be. It's a great way of doing it, but I am warning you about overdoing it. If you're a guy focused on delivering, then every time a new lead fades away or lets you down, you will find yourself backtracking, explaining what happened.

Trust and respect

(Aretha Franklin – Respect)

You should, in my humble opinion, aim for two basic things: To be trusted by colleagues and respected by adversaries.

People trust you will kick ass and bring home the money. Someone says "boy I am happy he is on the team".

As for adversaries, you should aim for respect when others look to you and say "oh oh they brought in their best guns, now we are in trouble". Because it's not a martial arts match very few times you will see or know the face of the adversaries, but rest assured they are there. You will know this from your first lost bid.

Set and meet expectations?

(Black Eyed Peas – I gotta feeling)

Expectations are about feelings. No sale is ever set in stone so it's also your gut feel talking when you are setting expectations or targets. It's how confident you are. I don't mean selling commodity products that sell on its own (in that case you're just a dispatcher, sorry).

A major sales leader in the aerospace business keeps promising and hitting his numbers year in and year out. This is far more difficult than it seems, and boils down to one simple fact. This person never sets impossible or unlikely expectations with the sales numbers. He is in control and only let slip what is a done deal or so near it could not slip.

I have failed to do this and learned the hard way when I also tweeted every single lead, presentation possibility or gossip throughout the company. With all good intentions so that people can be informed and look forward to exciting news. You have to strike a balance between keeping your mouth shut, and therefore closing yourself to the resources and push forward you may need, or wide open on every new bit of information, possibly demotivating people around you when it does not happen, and believe me more often than not.

Sales targets, bonuses and money

(Pink Floyd – Money)

One cannot write about sales and not talk about making money and bonuses. I am not even going to discuss the silly idea that salespeople make so much more money than everybody else, and because of that, many want to take a shot at it, some will not after reading this book...

Selling is also an attitude. Your attitude is influenced by many variables, one of them being your expectations of the future. If it involves money, for sure it will be in the forefront of your attention.

Some organizations provide sales bonuses to achieve certain targets and a percentage if you exceed it. Some other's don't, just a standard bonus.

I have lived both situations and while at the beginning they may feel the same, with time they are not. When you start mentally calculating the forecast of possible contracts and if you're likely to get that extra bonus, things will be prioritised differently.
Like everything in this world, there are up and down sides. If you do not have an incentive on the extra money, you will probably do a good

job and not stress yourself out with the sales quota, except if you're a guy that is concerned by your company's future.

But if you're going for gold, every victory feels like honey and every setback feels like sour milk.

The bottom line is that you should keep your cool and remember it's a marathon and not a sprint. If you're running fast just to achieve the short term objectives of getting some more money, you will for sure remember this chapter.

So the bottom line is that if you do well you can expect to reap rewards, but be prepared that it's a tough world and even if all goes well you may not get there. It may be that the target was too ambitious, or competition pulled an unexpected trick, or a major contract award was delayed indefinitely. Whatever impacts your bonus do not let it affect you. The organisation will be thankful and reward you if you do the best you can with a clear conscience.

If you can't make it alone, get help!

Again a hard learned lesson by the engineer convinced of its services superiority. Breaking into a new market or country is NOT easy. You may be pushing for a deal and doing your best, and all the stuff in this book and still can't get to first base with a potential customer. It can be very frustrating, time consuming and raise some questions internally about your effectiveness.

But here's what happens. As soon as you get some help, through a local partner or alliance, you get a little more attention (don't go crazy, it's just a bit, not a lot) and more traction.

That on its own is not enough, of course but it shows you should seriously think about all variables.

We tried to get a meeting at a major aerospace player for a long time, and given our niche expertise and geographical distance we simply could not get the invite to go over there. That was compounded with various people rotating in the procurement organisation, which meant that even if we were very very persistent, we always seem to be starting all over.

When we managed to put together a collaboration deal with a local company to present ourselves as a group, we finally managed to get the invite and present what we could do together.

But don't get too excited, that's just the beginning...

Humble

(REM – All the way to Reno)

There's no better defining characteristic than humility. In the same way no meeting is too short, no one can be too humble.
If you're an aspiring star, start with being nobody and one day you will see how to appreciate being appreciated.

Have a happy thought

(The Housemartins – Weather with you)

Be like Peter Pan, have a happy thought, even if you're afraid to fly. Your state of mind very much depends on how you react to adversity and tiredness. Focusing on something that puts a smile on your face definitely helps.

In the heat of the battle, sometimes you lose sight of happy thoughts, whether it's your family, your prized motorbike or having some pints with your mates.

Working hard and long hours tends to wear out your humour. This gets noticed and could transform into a snowball.

Take time out to get away, physically if needs to be, and DO NOT pay attention to what others may think. If you work and type better listening to music, then do it. Anything that makes you more productive and not strictly against company policies is worth doing.

If you need to unplug and have some piece of mind, never mind what others may think. Your productivity is what you get paid for and is the single most important variable in your daily work.

Behave!

Behaving is not just about being polite. It's about respecting the cultural differences, and you can be sure you will find many along the way, not just from country to country, but in different companies and clients.

Behaving means being alert and assertive to situations and reactions that could easily put you in the wrong foot with someone you're just starting off. It means accepting how others operate, even if you don't share that way of doing things, it means eating the food people put on the table (unless you have some allergy or vegetarian diet). It means observing the local rules of conduct and obeying the rules. Nobody wants to do business with rude people that ignore the way things are done locally.

Never forget

A few things to keep in mind when you go down the rabbit hole towards Wonderland.

Persistence, patience and politeness

(Guns n' Roses – Patience)

I find these 3 P's the cement for everything in sales:

Persistence, patience & politeness.

They should be self evident, but anyway....assumptions kills.

Persistence pays off eventually, see nearly all of the material in this book. If you haven't figured it out yet, please close now and ask for a refund. Perseverance is in fact the mother of all virtues.

The second P is for Patience. Patience is an overarching virtue, and one to be daily reinforced. All of this sales stuff can wear you out if you're not careful, in fact I have felt like it numerous times, but always rebounded somehow. I guess most of the times it was just by taking conscience of these lessons learned.

Politeness is a basic human quality. You will get people being aggressive, you will see people behaving improperly, breaking commitments, badmouthing and the list can go on. You should NEVER lose your politeness, unless you are under physical distress or imminent danger. Otherwise suck it in if you need to (I am still working at this, I could never tolerate rude people even if they are customers).

On this last point, sometimes politeness is not what is in the book. Cultural sensitivities can affect how someone sees you being polite or not. This is actually looking at internal customers, as they will be more "touchy feely", and you of course will talk to them in a more natural and direct way. This can be hard to manage, if you're hardwired for achieving objectives. Sometimes giving simple and direct instructions hurts sensitivities and people will see you in a not so good way.

Never never give up!

(Sheryl Crow – All I wanna do)

All I wanna do is…is to give up…many times it will cross your head. I don't mean altogether but slowly letting it go quietly.

I know this is Winston's Churchill phrase, but I'd like to borrow it as I also live daily with this motto. More than a lesson, it's a philosophy. One of my bosses had this great picture of a frog going down the throat of a stork, with his "hands" choking the neck, not giving up and battling while being eaten alive.

You must have a good gut to suffer daily minor setbacks, delays and other discouraging events. Winners never quit.

Remember that awesome project you were going to present and last minute, sorry it's postponed indefinitely. Your morale is down; you feel like having a drink. But you don't do that. Give the customer thanks for the opportunity. Write it down for whatever period of time you find convenient to resume and follow up. In 6 months time, next thing you know you're doing it.

In many many situations you will be pushing sand uphill, the odds are against you, you're bidding when you know there is a lobby or a group very likely to win, but you DO NOT back off. Just say to yourself giving up is not an option and manage your life accordingly!

Trigger happy

(Therapy – Trigger inside)

There will be times when someone will send you an email or call you with arguments or replies that will get your blood pumping.

Your first reaction, as most of us, will be to read and re-read the email and reply each sentence and each point. Especially when it's something that you strongly oppose or disagree altogether you feel that urge to tell'em with adrenalyn included.

BUT, as you know, many emails are badly written, misunderstood or the person writing It does not have a clear mind or understanding at the topic at hand. So you get all trigger happy and the email fight begins, likely putting others in copy or blind copy.

Here's one piece of advice, no matter how hard it may seem, and I have really learned it the hard way: if you want to reply and blow off steam, write it BUT don't send it. Ask others for opinions or views if what you understood and plan to reply is actually in line with reality. If it can wait for the next day, it's a great opportunity to sleep on it, read again your draft and adjust the tone if needed.

I once received an email about workshare, pricing etc from a company which we were working together on a project. Our relationship to date was not excellent but we got along with some reserves from both sides. Then this emails pops in full of what I considered lies and incorrect facts and it was really a cry for war for me. I must have written one of the harshest emails ever but managed to follow my rule and leave it simmering overnight. While the next day did not bring any new light on the subjec, I did manage to discuss it with others involved and tone it down to what we believed was more appropriate rather than to start an email (and possible corporate) fight.

Know when to fight and when to fold

(Tracy Chapman - Born to fight)

This is actually not my idea, and not in contradiction with "never give up". It's more like postponing in a temporary manner.

You can't win them all; in fact you only win some or even few. But you should know when to retreat.

Especially during follow up you can get caught in the excitement and anxiety of pushing forward that you can get yourself into a situation producing the opposite result. If the "fight is off" because the project is delayed, don't be a pain and fold it for awhile. Then plan your come back to action.

Or in more extreme cases, if the contract is already assigned to a competitor, you can try to jump the line and do a counter bid, but if they have signed the contract, why are you wasting your time?

Getting closer?

(Sheryl Crow - Everyday is a winding road...)

"Everyday is a winding road, I get a little bit closer" is a daily constant. If you're an impatient guy like me (I used to be more to be honest) you have to hum all the time this tune to cool you off. Every action, campaign or negotiation is just like that, a long and winding road without a clear end in sight, but you've got to walk down that road to bring you closer to your goals.

Having spent quite some years in programme management, where planning is central, I have never seen ANY plan being exactly met or followed without any changes along the road. It is hard to get in your "junior manager operating system" to accept your plans are useless without going through it. As someone said, "It is the act of planning, not the plans, that are important".

Now translate this into sales. Plan as much as you want...First of all, when a customer lays out a set of proposal and project milestones, they will in 99% of the cases change them, and I'm just talking about delivering the proposal, never mind the actual execution (aerospace has a really bad track record of following plans). Then you have your expectations about when you will know something about winning or not, before going into final negotiations about price, reviewing contract clauses and putting together the team.
And that leads again to...patience. Don't play solitary or any other procrastinating activity; reorganize your folders, review old leads and get as productive as you can. USE it to think and reflect about what you could have done better. Write it down if you want to.

Taking on the world

(Gun – Taking on the world)

All of this pitching and dealing will surely take you up and down an emotional rollercoaster. Sometimes you will feel like "Highlander" where you can take on any challenge, or some other times you will feel down in a hole.

This will be especially true when you win or lose big.

I once worked on a big contract for 6 months and the whole company up to the managing director was involved and anxious to see if we would win it. We did a great job but in the end we lost out to a consulting company which was far bigger and better known than we were, so despite of the great battle, we fell.
This was heart breaking for me as I felt personally responsible for what happened. After all, if you're leading the sales campaigns should you not be? I reflected on this for some time and at first noticed nobody wanted to mention it in the aftermath, perhaps afraid of my "hurt feelings" about losing a major contract. I guess it was something else. Remember they were also very keen on winning and also worked equally hard. So they were equally disappointed.

The moral of the story is that sales executives must take face for good or worse, but don't put the weight of the world on your shoulders. Remember that it's not your win; it's the company's, even if you are proud of winning or taking responsibility for the loss.

Never lose hope, but expect the worse?

(The Verve – Bittersweet symphony)

Persistence and following up are closely linked to hope, and most importantly not losing it. If you end up in a string of contacts and rebounds from person to person eventually it starts to wear you out, and your hopes or expectations will be affected.

It may seem a paradox to you, but the best way not to lose hope is not to have it in the first place. It's cooling down your unlimited optimism to a level of tranquillity if something ends up not the way you expected.

Passion is needed and a great asset, but if you take every setback and defeat personally, you will suffer a lot. If you manage to cool down your expectations, it's like developing a thicker skin for absorbing impacts.

To win you must learn to lose

It is impossible to know how to win without losing. Even the greatest athletes, business people and many other professions once lost a competition, a deal or support from someone. In the same way that some people say that dying is part of your life; losing is part of the winning process. This truly is "learning on the job" and cannot be taught independently. And remember, winners never quit!

"Busyness"

All high powered executives have this aura of "maxed out" agendas, and how little time they have to talk to or meet people.

It also happens that it's much more convenient to be "busy" by default than to be available instantly. That's sort of a built in protection people use not to be bothered, so be wary when someone's agenda does not allow even for 15 minutes talk. They are either genuinely "work machines" or they are very selective and avoiding you.

From your own working perspective, yes we are all "busy" with peaks and valleys, but in general you should be ALWAYS available to help. I don't mean not sleeping because you are buried in useless requests (that's something else, knowing how to say no), but making an effort towards a colleague or a client. Trust me, one day you too will need someone to help you out on matters important and trivial alike.

Be inquisitive about WIP

(Iron Maiden – Fear of the dark)

I cannot remember how many times I have heard from colleagues in various jobs that "it's ongoing".

Be very wary when someone says this. Most of the times they are clueless about what the real progress is, and this is the point where you need to be extra inquisitive, in an assertive way, very hard to do I know.

Sales are not just the networking, travelling and finding ways to pitch. It's also hard work; paperwork and teamwork (note the repetition of the word "work"). This means you must revert to managerial skills most often unused while in full sales mode.

Because when you finally have that RFP to answer, you need to reply in the best possible way.

This means understanding the structure of the document, how to organize it, assign parts to relevant people in the company and set milestones.

A great feedback I once had totally unexpected was from a senior manager that was particularly nice, to the point of being a bit on the "naive" side. She said "Pedro, I think you will be a good manager as you don't take things on face value". What she saw in me was the capacity of questioning and challenging the status quo. Be careful about this as different countries and working cultures have different views on this, as I learned the hard way...

Anything worthwhile takes time and effort

If you find yourself thinking things are moving too slowly or that a certain task demands a lot of effort, breathe long and deep. We all know it in our gut that good things come to those who wait, but waiting is not enough on its own, you must sweat it out. If you want to lose weight, get educated or anything else worthwhile YOU must take the time and effort to make it happen.

This goes for writing a good proposal, researching another company, networking (this one demands a plan!), and pretty much anything you want to do properly.

When I first started doing business development my worse enemy was always my patience. I could never figure out why things moved so slowly or why people did not respond to simple requests. It takes time to adapt to the "rhythm" of a certain industry. If "Fast Moving Consumer Group" says it all, then others are more of the opposite and could easily be called "Long and delayed Manufacturing industry"!

Well, you may not like it and honestly do your best to change it, but don't set yourself for failure. You alone can exert some small influence (in a limited way), but not change an industry overnight...

When everything fails, work even harder!

(Louis Armstrong – What a wonderful world)

After all the persistence, patience and drive you have in you, be sure that things will not go to plan and will fail more often than not. Don't be discouraged about the immediate results (it's a marathon, not a sprint, remember?) or the aftermath of some sales campaigns. You need to have a fighting spirit and keep going, so just do the best thing you can do: work even harder! That's right, you can always do it better and harder, no matter how good you are doing it already. Times of dissapointment tend to promote reflection on how things are going and probably will give you new ideas to improve your way of working.

And...it never ends

The job itself, if done properly never ends, so don't plan too much or get frustrated. The good news is that you will always be learning new lessons simply because the world, and especially sales, is a dynamic environment. Let's just say that this book is a pause in time with my reflections to date, surely many more to come which I hope to share with you one day again.

www.ingramcontent.com/pod-product-compliance
Lightning Source LLC
Chambersburg PA
CBHW060623210326
41520CB00010B/1453